Travelling to My Island Home, Thursday Island

By Matilda Loban

Illustrated by Keishart

Library For All Ltd.

I come from an island at the top of the land Down Under, where beautiful coconut trees grow tall and strong.

To get to my island home, you need to take many types of transport.

Sometimes, I have to be brave and travel alone to visit my family.

On school holidays, I travel from Cairns to Thursday Island.

At the airport, I meet a flight attendant and she gives me a tag to put on my shirt, so the staff know who I am and how to contact my family. She gets me safely on the plane.

As I get closer to the Torres Strait from Cairns airport, I can see the clear, bright blue water.

I get excited as I know I'm flying home.

As the plane lands on Horn Island, I step out on to the tarmac, and I'm greeted with the thick humidity.

I am welcomed on to Kaurareg Country by the traditional custodians of that land.

As I take the small trip from the airport to the wharf, where we catch the ferry, I look out the window at my surroundings. As we drive, I see the bushland, and the island sand mixed with the dirt of the Far North.

Once I arrive at the wharf, the fresh salty air of the water hits my nose and throat, and I know I am even closer to home.

I take my luggage down to the wharf and board the ferry. Waving goodbye to Horn Island, I hear the waves crash against the boat as it goes faster and faster towards Thursday Island.

As we dock at Thursday Island, I hear the seagulls singing overhead, watching the fish in the clear blue water. I see my mum standing, waving, ready to embrace me in a huge hug.

Her little island girl is almost home.

The last part of my journey home is in the back seat of our car. We take a lap around the island to remind me of the people and the places I remember.

I love coming back to my island home, Thursday Island.

Travelling to Thursday Island.

You can use these questions to talk about this book with your family, friends and teachers.

What did you learn from this book?

Describe this book in one word. Funny? Scary? Colourful? Interesting?

How did this book make you feel when you finished reading it?

What was your favourite part of this book?

Download the Library For All Reader app from libraryforall.org

About the author

Matilda was born in Cairns. She was raised between Thursday Island and Townsville, and currently calls Thursday Island home. Her language group is Kala Lagaw Ya. She enjoys yarning with her family and telling her children stories of when she grew up. Her favourite stories as a child were traditional ones shared by the family.

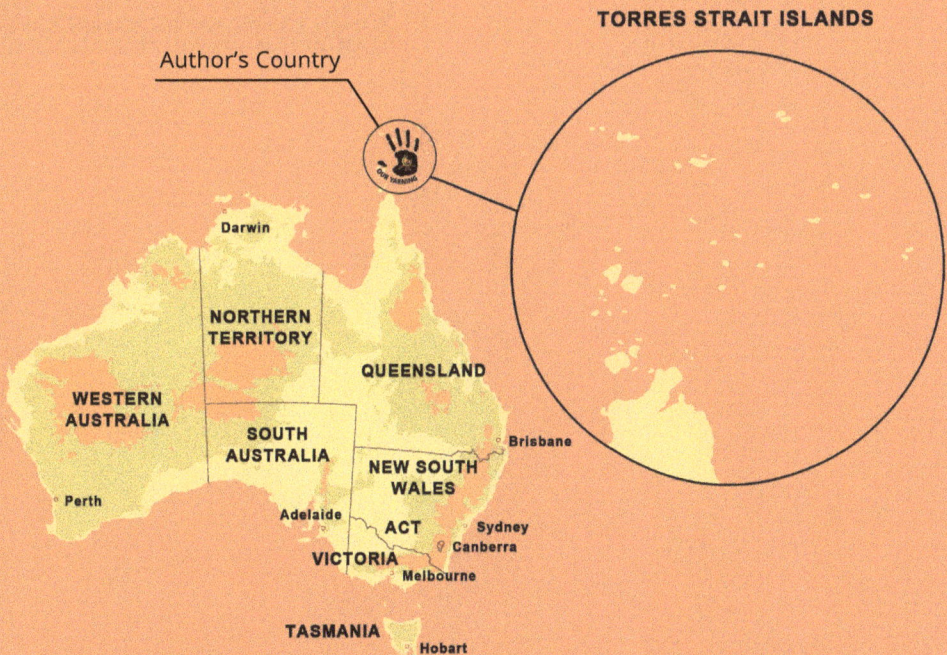

TORRES STRAIT ISLANDS

Author's Country

Darwin

NORTHERN
TERRITORY

QUEENSLAND

WESTERN
AUSTRALIA

SOUTH
AUSTRALIA

NEW SOUTH
WALES

Perth

Brisbane

Adelaide

ACT

Sydney
Canberra

VICTORIA

Melbourne

TASMANIA

Hobart

Our Yarning

The Our Yarning collection aligns with the Australian Curriculum through the Cross-Curriculum Priorities — Aboriginal and Torres Strait Islander Histories and Cultures. The collection provides an authentic opportunity for learning and embedding Aboriginal and Torres Strait Islander perspectives because it is written by Aboriginal and Torres Strait Islander people.

We know that children learn better, and enjoy reading more, when they see themselves in the stories, characters and illustrations of the books they read.

To download the app, visit the Google Play Store or Apple Store and search 'Our Yarning'.

librayforall.org

You're reading Level 4

Learner – Beginner readers
Start your reading journey with short words, big ideas and plenty of pictures.

Level 1 – Rising readers
Raise your reading level with more words, simple sentences and exciting images.

Level 2 – Eager readers
Enjoy your reading time with familiar words, but complex sentences.

Level 3 – Progressing readers
Develop your reading skills with creative stories and some challenging vocabulary.

Level 4 – Fluent readers
Step up your reading skills with playful narratives, new words and fun facts.

Middle Primary – Curious readers
Discover your world through science and stories.

Upper Primary – Adventurous readers
Explore your world through science and stories.

Library For All is an Australian not for profit organisation with a mission to make knowledge accessible to all via an innovative digital library solution. Visit us at libraryforall.org

Travelling to My Island Home, Thursday Island

First published 2024

Published by Library For All Ltd
Email: info@libraryforall.org
URL: libraryforall.org

Our Yarning logo design by Jason Lee, Bidjipidji Art

Original illustrations by Keishart

Travelling to My Island Home, Thursday Island
Loban, Matilda
ISBN: 978-1-923207-18-9
SKU04395